Instagram Marketing

——— ✦✦✦ ———

Using Instagram Social Media To Amplify Your Business And Brand Visibility

By Logan King

Table of Contents

Introduction

I want to congratulate and thank you for choosing my book "Instagram Marketing: Using Instagram Social Media To Amplify Your Business And Brand Visibility!"

Let me just start by informing you that Instagram is quickly dominating the social media circles and every brand worth its salt has started making use of Instagram widely to gain the attention of potential customers.

After all, why wouldn't they? It has been proven time and again that we remember what we see most vividly, and Instagram is completely based on sharing photos and videos.

So in this book, we're going to learn about how you can use this amazing platform to increase the visibility of your business, reach out to potential customers and profit from it.

So without further ado, let's get started.

Chapter 1:

Instagram For Business

Instagram is no longer just a pastime or hobby for people spending time online. It has developed into a huge platform for making money, promoting businesses and other marketing agendas. While Instagram itself does not buy or sell anything, millions of users make use of Instagram services to make income and earn money.

From small businesses to the topmost international brands, everyone promotes their business on Instagram. Ever since online shopping became the norm, marketing on Instagram became even more revolutionary. Marketing on Instagram is easy and accessible to everyone worldwide.

Here's how you can promote your business on Instagram:

- Get a separate account for your business and keep it clear of any personal information. It is just the same as a personal account, the only difference being that all your posts are going to be business-centric.

- Your posts should be in accordance with the demand of the customers. While promoting your business, you should also be able to entertain the users and hold their interest with your posts.

- When promoting your products, capture them in such a way that they look desirable to the customers. Educate your customers about their benefits and merits and why they must have those products.

- Your pictures should be creative and crisp. Take multiple shots of the products from different angles until you get the perfect shot and then upload it. Keep the background clean; use a good camera and sharper lenses. The graphics must be of high resolution. When your products show aesthetic beauty, they are more likely to pique the interest of potential customers.

- Build themes. Themes are a great way to let people know what you have to offer and what they should expect when following your account.

- To expand your customer base, you've got to have more followers and likes on your posts. Using hash tags and interacting with other users are some easy ways to do that. We will discuss how to get a maximum number of likes and followers in detail in the following chapters.

- Advertise your business with the help of videos. Videos are more efficient in promotion as they hold the attention of the customers for longer. You can directly upload videos on Instagram or share them via YouTube and other website links.

- Be consistent in posting. Don't post too frequently as it may spam your customers' feeds. Neither should you take too long before posting, rather you should keep your activities in balance. Prepare a schedule for posting and post at regular intervals. There are certain times of day and night when the traffic on Instagram is maximum, so post during this time to get the maximum number of likes.

- While Instagram has a nice collection of tools for editing pictures and videos, there are other applications in app stores that are specifically built for the purpose of editing. Make use of these applications to make your pictures attractive and then share them on Instagram. Use filters, adjust lighting, contrast, brightness, sharpness and other features to give your photographs a desirable look.

- Let your customers know that you appreciate them. You can do this by posting customer-centric posts, thanking them in your posts and replying to their comments and queries on your posts. When you interact frequently with your customers, this forms a loyal relationship between the customers and the business.

- Share the events and activities that take place at your workplace with your customers such as a gathering or any celebrations. This makes a good impression of your business.

Benefits of Using Instagram for Marketing

Along with personal use, Instagram is a useful tool for promoting business and marketing as well. In some ways, marketing through Instagram is much easier and convenient in comparison with some other platforms. There are some benefits that only Instagram can provide or provides better than the others. Let us discuss what these benefits are.

- Customers prefer to have a visual of the products before they make the decision to buy them. Since Instagram is the most convenient social networking platform for sharing photos and videos, it is perfect for marketing. You can upload images of your products on Instagram along with their description and purchase links that make it very convenient for business.

- You can tease the customers by sharing glimpses and giving small hints about the new products that are going to be launched in the future.

- Marketing on Instagram is absolutely free of cost. Instagram does not charge the businesses for the promotion of their products. Their services are free to use for everyone. This of course leads to a lot of competition in the field of marketing, but as long as you give your customers enough reasons to go with your company, you have nothing to worry about. The money these businesses save from using Instagram services for free can be utilized in other ways such as developing more creative concepts for advertisement.

- Instagram makes it easier for businesses and customers to interact with each other. Businesses can share how their products are manufactured in the factories, what type of material is being used and how the manufacturers work, with their customers. This results in a loyal customer base.

- You can ask for favors from other popular Instagram accounts to promote your business on their profiles. This is a fast and efficient way to direct traffic towards your business account. In return you can promote their businesses or even pay them.

Chapter 2:

Getting Started On Instagram

Instagram is an online platform for posting and viewing photographs and thus can be accessed on any device with an Internet connection and suitable browsers, but Instagram is best suited for mobile phones and tablets through the official Instagram app which is a complete package of all the features available on Instagram.

You can download the Instagram app on your iOS and Android devices from their respective app stores.

To get started on Instagram, one must first register. To create an Instagram account, the user has to select a username that is not already taken and create their own password. After that, the user is required to fill in their personal details such as a display name, gender and an email address to associate with the account.

It is also optional for the user to add their mobile number to their Instagram profile. After that, there comes the need for a profile picture. These profile details can be changed at any time.

There is also an option for writing a bio description for your profile. The character limit for a bio is set to be 150 characters, but it can be left blank as per the convenience and will of the user. Another very helpful feature on Instagram is the space provided for entering a websites link in your profile.

This link can be accessed by anyone who visits that user's profile. Websites links are very helpful in promoting businesses online and this makes Instagram an efficient marketing platform.

Any Instagram profile and all their posts are available for public viewing by default, but there are options for making a profile private. When an Instagram account is private, anyone who wishes to view the posts on that account will have to send that user a follow request, and they will only be able to follow their posts when the follower request is accepted.

Approving or declining the follower requests is in the power of the owner of the concerned profile alone.

Notifications

You can choose how you want to be notified of the activities on your account. These notifications will pop up automatically under the news tab when you're using the Instagram app. However, to get notifications externally when the app is not in direct use, the push notifications function is also available in the app.

You can toggle your app settings to turn the push notifications function on. While using the app, you can tell the nature of the notification by recognizing the notification bubbles that appear right over the news tab of the app. A heart bubble represents a like on one of your posts, while a speech bubble represents a comment.

There is also a separate notification bubble for when someone tags you in a picture or for when you receive a new follower or a new follower request in case of a private account. Instagram also lets you know when you've been mentioned in a comment or in one of the posts by other pages on Instagram.

Connecting with the world

Since Instagram is officially a social networking app, the main idea of Instagram is to connect with people from all across of the world. Instagram provides you with the feature to link your Instagram account with your Facebook, Twitter, Foursquare, Flickr, Mixi, Weibo, Tumblr or VK account.

This feature is available in the sharing settings and you can also choose to share your posts on the linked profiles when making a post on the Instagram. Just select which profile and click post and your picture will be posted on your Instagram feed as well as on the linked profiles. The privacy settings on your Instagram still hold even when you share your posts on the linked profiles.

Posting Graphical Media

All the posts on Instagram are necessarily in the form of photos and videos. The nature and content of the photos and videos is important in promoting the businesses. Here's a step-by-step guide for uploading photographs and videos on Instagram.

The moment you tap the add button in the center of the panel in the Instagram app, the app allows you to choose whether you want to upload a photo or video newly taken by the camera or choose an already existing one from the device's storage.

Just simply tap the button and the app will have access to your device's camera and shoot your photos and videos. The time limit set by the Instagram for video uploading is a duration of a minimum of 3 seconds, which can be extended up to 60 seconds. You have to keep your finger pressed on the record button for as long as you want to record the video within the set duration limits.

You can also record videos in small segments by simply taking your finger off the record button when you want to stop recording and then tapping it again when you want to resume the recording process.

To post the media already existing in your device's storage, you'll have to swipe left from the camera screen in Instagram. This will take you to the camera roll and all the existing pictures and videos will be available to you in one place for selection and upload.

If there is any trouble in locating the media you want to upload on Instagram, you can narrow your search to the specific folder your media is located in from the drop down list that shows all the media containing folders in your device.

Photos and videos cropped in the dimensions of a square are most fitted for upload otherwise you may or may not have to crop your content before uploading (for example, in the case of pictures and videos having marginally more length than width).

Making posts look attractive

You can choose to upload your media as it is in the original form, but when it comes to marketing and promoting businesses, it is important to make your content look attractive and appealing to the viewer. Remember, you wouldn't want to change your media so much that it totally stops resembling the real thing but a little touch up wouldn't go amiss.

Now Instagram provides a plethora of tools to achieve that feat and edit your content as best as possible. You can start with the amazing collection of filters Instagram has to offer. These filters can have a pleasant effect on the whole vibe of your content.

You can apply these filters in their default form. In case that doesn't work out for you, you can modify these filters to lighten or deepen the filter effect. Other than the filters, there are other options too which are in the following order- 'Adjust' for rotating and adjusting the pictures, 'Brightness' for adjusting the brightness, 'Contrast' for increasing or decreasing the contrast, Structure, Warmth, Saturation, Color, Fade, Highlights, Shadows, Vignette, Tilt Shift and Sharpening.

Another feature that is the lux effect is also a pretty attractive feature that automatically enhances the image. Its depth can be altered. All of these features can be applied to your pictures and their degrees can be varied, best suited to your needs.

Instagram Filters

We briefly mentioned the wide variety of filters Instagram provide to its users. For your business to flourish, it is important that your content on Instagram looks appealing to the viewers, and for that purpose filters are important tools. They can modify and enhance the look of your photos and make them look prettier and more attractive.

Now your most important concern is to select a filter that best suits your picture. For this selection, you must first know what attributes each filter enhances in your picture so you can choose what you want based on that information. Given below is a brief to-the-point description of each Instagram filter.

- **Normal**: Normal displays the original picture without any filters applied on it. Click on normal to revert back to the default picture when you wish to remove a filter.

- **Lo-Fi**: This filter comprises of enhanced warmth of the temperature in the picture and a prominent spike in the Saturation levels. This works to bring out the shadows in a stark contrast and the colors feel richer.

- **Earlybird**: With increased warmth and a sepia tint, this filter introduces a hint of the olden days to the picture.

- **Amaro**: This filter enhances the light at the center of the picture along with a deepened focus.

- **Rise**: Soft lights and a noticeable glow are the distinct features of this filter that sets it apart from other filters.

- **Inkwell**: By applying this filter, your colored picture will turn into a black and white picture.

- **Sutro**: On application of this filter, you will find that the picture is more highlighted, shadows are enhanced, the edges are touched with a burnt look and purple and brown parts of the picture become more prominent.

- **Mayfair**: With this filter, the picture is touched with a vignette effect at the edges that in turn makes the center of the picture glow with an attractive brightness. The whole picture is overlaid by a pinkish effect and you'll also see a thin black border around it.

- **Sierra**: The filter enhances the photograph by making use of the fade effect, providing the picture a softer appearance.

- **Valencia**: The increase of intensity of the exposure levels and warmth in the picture is what gives this filter its distinct identity. The overall effects give an antique look to the picture.

- **Nashville**: A feeling of nostalgia strikes on the application of this filter. With its soft pink tint and low contrast along with high temperature and exposure levels, this filter becomes a great choice.

- **Toaster**: Again, there is a vignette effect at the edges of the picture while the center is modified with a burnt effect.

- **Perpetua**: The filter 'Perpetua' gives the picture a pastel look and hence is a popular and useful tool.

- **X-Pro**: With vibrant colors, enhanced contrast, a golden touch and the application of the vignette effect at the borders of the image, X-Pro is a beautiful filter.

- **Cream**: As the name goes, this filter provides the picture with a creamy look. There is a prominent modification of warmth too.

- **Walden**: Enhanced exposure levels in the picture and a subtle yellow color tint are the distinct features of this filter.

- **Aden**: This filter has a noticeable effect on the blue and green sections of the image; color tints are visible too.

- **Slumber**: The black and blue sections of the image become richer and the saturation levels drop on the application of this filter.

- **Ludwig**: More light and less Saturation are the most prominent characteristics of this filter.

Apart from the above-mentioned filters, there are some other filters too. If you already know what you want for your picture, you can directly select your filter of choice. Otherwise, you can try out each filter and see what suits your preferences best. Each filter has a distinct set of features that sets it apart from the others so choosing from them should not be too hard.

Sharing

After you've edited your image and chosen the preferred filter, you proceed to the sharing screen. Here Instagram allows you to write a caption for your image or video. You can also use hash tags in the caption that make it easier for the viewers to look up your posts when they explore under those hash tags. To mention another profile in your posts, simply write '@' and the username of the user you wish to mention.

You can also tag other users in your posts on this screen, again by tapping on the image where you wish to tag them and then typing their username. Turning on the location will share the location of the picture with the viewers.

If you wish to share your posts to the linked profiles, simply tap the ones you wish to share with and your posts will be shared on those profiles with the same caption. This feature is available at the time of posting and also after the post has been made.

Instagram Direct

This feature was later introduced into the Instagram app. With this feature, videos and images can be shared between two users but cannot be viewed by anyone other than the selected users. After that, another feature of direct messaging was introduced too. This feature can prove great for direct interaction with customers.

Chapter 3:

Making Your Instagram Account Appealing

Getting popularity on Instagram is no easy task, but if you know how to play your cards right, you will find that this task isn't too hard either. All you need is to do is attract the right crowd and the way to ensure that is by making your Instagram account and the content on it attractive.

Now remember, like every other area, there is a great deal of competition on Instagram too and to make an impression, you will have to become the best. The shortest way towards popularity is posting the right content at the right time. Let us list some of the measures you can take to make sure you leave a lasting impression on the minds of viewers.

For an attractive Instagram profile, the username must be attractive. Most of the viewers notice the username first thing when they visit an Instagram profile. You should refrain from using too many symbols in username, they might make the profile appear unprofessional or scare users into thinking it is a scam.

The next step is to put a picture on display that best suits your agenda. If your profile is personal, go for a pic of yourself. For business profiles, use a profile picture of your business's logo or watermark. Never leave the profile picture empty; it may make your account look unauthentic.

Build Themes

Set a theme for your account. Themes are important for the success of an Instagram profile because when your page has a particular theme, the visitors will know what your account has to offer and what they should expect when visiting your profile. You can choose your theme depending on your business and the important part is to own it.

Pick up a theme and make the best of it. Basically, consistency is the key. For example if you own a food business, make a theme full of food items, post pictures that will make any food lover's mouth water. If it's about clothing and fashion, set a theme that showcases the best of fashion world. If it's about travel, have a theme that is focused on popular places, exotic landscapes, mountainsides, riversides and wherever your business has roots. Follow a pattern such as posting all the pictures on your page in black & white or sepia, or giving them a certain colored tint.

A good theme will make your profile look attractive and make an overall good impression. This is likely to get you a large number of followers and make your Instagram account popular.

Now that you've an idea what your theme is going to be, the next step is to post good relevant pictures. An empty profile may be able to generate traffic by any means but the chances of getting genuine followers decrease when there is no content to see on the profile.

To avoid that, you should put together a portfolio with the best pictures which will set good standards for your business and people would want to follow you in expectations of even better content. The pictures you post must be of high quality. Good lighting, nice background, good visuals, a good camera and suitable editing. All these combined will give your pictures a rich look and get the attention of your followers.

You must make sure the pictures you are posting are not irrelevant or of bad quality, because that will give a bad look to your page. Quality over quantity should be your mantra. You may have to make extra effort to get the perfect shot and the process may take time or several tries, but it's all worth it when the pictures reach the right crowd.

Sometimes, stock editing tools on Instagram may not be enough for the desirable effect you want for your pictures and in that case you can also use the help of other editing applications for editing your pictures as there are plenty of them available in the app stores. They are built specifically for the purpose of editing and may have more efficient tools than Instagram. Use them to give your pictures the look you desire and then proceed to post them on your Instagram.

Captions can play a great role in making a good impression of your posts. It is normal behavior to read captions after viewing a photograph or video. When your captions are catchy and smart, people will find it easier to relate your content. Your caption may be a simple description of the picture or a quote that hits something deep in the mind or just simple facts about the content in the picture, or anything else as long as it bears some relevance to the picture.

Chapter 3: Making Your Instagram Account Appealing

Too lengthy and bland captions can be boring and uninteresting so you may want to read the caption to yourself first and decide if it's interesting enough before posting.

Add a personal touch to your profile. There is a lot of competition in the business marketing on Instagram. While professionalism is good, too much professionalism will make your account appear robotic, as if there is no human behind the account. To hold the interest of your viewers, your job is to provide the viewers with something that other pages do not have, and that is your own personal flavor.

This will allow your followers to form a connection with you. There is some story to each picture; all you have to do is share the stories behind your posts with your followers, your personal experiences and opinions and how you feel about the content of your post.

To get more followers, you can link your Instagram with other social media profiles such as Twitter, Facebook, Tumblr, Foursquare and those outlined in a previous chapter. This is a great way to get people to follow you. You can promote your Instagram account on these profiles and share your post links.

If you have a famous blog, Facebook, Tumblr or other accounts, mention your Instagram account there and ask people to give it a follow. This will notify your contacts on other networks of your Instagram account and make it easier for them to follow and connect with you on Instagram although you will have to give them a reason to follow your Instagram profile.

Keep your Instagram posts unique and interesting and set them apart from your posts on other profiles. This way, people will follow you in anticipation of seeing something more than they have already seen.

The best way to go about getting a huge amount of likes and followers is to like and follow others first. Mostly everyone's motive on Instagram is to get as many likes and followers as they can. Your job is to get people to notice you and this can be done by liking and commenting on their posts and following them.

Once they get your notification, they may check you out too and like your posts or even follow you. If you do not want to follow too many users, just stick to liking and commenting. You can also analyze and learn from other popular accounts relating to the same kind of business as yours. Go through their following and followers lists; you are more likely to find users there who are already interested in the type of your business. Get their attention by liking and commenting on their posts.

Direct interaction with other users is a great way to go about making connections. Comments are more likely to get noticed than likes, even more so when your comments are flattering. If you manage to win them with your comments, they may check out your posts and follow you in the best-case scenario.

Also you should never ignore the comments on your posts. Make a point of replying to each and every comment and enquiry on your posts to let the users know that you appreciate them. Otherwise they may feel reluctant to comment on your posts in the future. This will make a good impression of your account in the Instagram community.

Start Using Hashtags

To increase the reach of your posts, you can make use of hash tags. Using hash tags is the easiest way to make sure that your posts reach out to those who would be genuinely interested in them. Instagram users mostly search for their desired content under relevant hash tags, your job is to know which hash tags these are and mention them in your posts. Make sure that these hash tags are related to your posts.

This method is even more efficient when you use the most popular hash tags. Searching for popular hash tags on Instagram is an easy task as suggestions automatically become visible when you start typing out a hash tag along with the total count of posts these hash tags have been used in.

Once you've managed to gain a good following, you can organize contests for your followers. You can set conditions for participation in these contests such as anyone who wishes to participate must follow your account or like your posts or tag your account in their posts. This will increase the reach of your page and get you more followers and likes.

Do not spam the feeds of your followers. This may cause them annoyance and get them to unfollow you. Quality over quantity should be your main aim. Make sure you leave some time between your posts and do not repeat them. Closely timed posts are highly likely to get overlooked and get fewer likes. Therefore, you should only post at regular intervals and each one of your posts should be different from the previous ones.

Certain types of pictures and videos get more attention than the rest, your job is to find out which pictures these are and post more of their preference. This way, your page may become popular faster. While sticking to the theme of your account is important, exceptions can be made in some cases.

For example, pictures set in natural landscapes, night times, cleaner backgrounds, sunrises and sunsets, water pictures and such get more likes than others. So make good use of your camera and get creative.

Another factor that has a direct effect on the reach of your posts is the privacy settings of your account. A private account has very few chances of getting popular, as their posts are only visible to their followers and not to the rest of the Instagram community.

Most users make the decision of following a page by the content of the user's posts, but in case of private accounts, the posts become hidden to them and this poses an obstacle in that decision-making. Business related accounts should be kept public for viewing or they may not be able to expand their database as quickly as they want.

The bio on your profile should be catchy and attractive enough to pique the interest of the visitors. In your bio, you can mention the nature of your business and what you have to offer so the readers can know what to expect when following your account.

Chapter 4:

How to Get Likes on Your Instagram

L ikes are equivalent of positive feedback when it comes to Instagram. The more likes your posts have, the more you know that your business is getting the attention it needs. The main idea of posting pictures on Instagram is to get likes, be it a personal profile or a business one.

When your posts have too few likes, it reflects badly on your profile and makes a bad impression to onlookers. In this chapter, we are going to help you learn some simple tricks to get more likes on your Instagram posts.

1. The first trick to get more likes is by getting more followers. More followers mean your posts are going to reach more people and that means more likes. To get more followers, you can link your Instagram with other social media profiles such as Twitter, Facebook, Tumblr, Foursquare and such as outlined in a previous chapter. Use these platforms to promote your Instagram account. Post your Instagram link on these profiles and share your posts there via the Instagram sharing feature. If you have an influential blog, Facebook, Tumblr or other accounts, mention your

Instagram account there and request people to give it a follow. This will notify your contacts on other networks of your Instagram account and make it easier for them to follow and connect with you on Instagram. Although, you will have to give them a reason to follow your Instagram profile. Keep your Instagram posts unique and interesting and keep them different from your posts on other profiles. This way, people will follow you in the hope of seeing even better content than they have already seen. These people are going to be your first followers and are likely to like your posts.

2. Good high definition pictures and videos are more likely to pique the interest of your viewers as opposed to any bad quality ones. Furthermore, it sets good standards for your page and people will follow you in anticipation of better content in the future. As we established above, more followers mean more likes.

3. Add a personal touch to your posts; you do not want your Instagram to look like a ghost account. Your personal experiences, opinions and comments will set your account apart from other business-related accounts and attract the attention of users worldwide.

4. The next trick is to use hash tags in your posts. People often look for their desired content by searching under the related hash tags so they can see all of it in one place. Your job is to put the most used and popular hash tags that relate to the content of your pictures in the captions of your posts so they can become widely visible to more number of users. You must know which hash tags are in trend and use them. Instagram is very helpful in this area as the suggestions become visible when you type '#' and the keywords with the total

count of posts in which those hash tags have been used. The more people your posts reach out to, the more likes they get.

5. A well-edited picture or video is supposedly more likely to get more likes. This depends on the picture to be posted and the owner of the post. Some pictures look better as they naturally are while others can use a touch of editing. Use filters, make use of the tools Instagram has to offer and make your picture as best as it can be. Some of the most used and liked filters are Hefe, Valencia and Earlybird.

6. Direct interaction with other users on Instagram is another trick to lure their attention to your profile that may lead to them checking out your posts, liking them or even following you. Comment on the posts from other accounts, so the owner of that account and other users who read your comments may notice you.

7. There are certain hash tags such as #LikeForLike, #FollowForFollow and #SpamForSpam and users who use these hash tags are more likely to follow and like your posts. It is like asking a favor in return for a favor. You get likes and follows in return for liking and following. To make sure you get noticed, like and comment on enough of their posts so your notifications don't get overlooked. Everyone on Instagram wants as many likes and follows as they can get, so it is one of the easiest and most efficient methods.

8. You may have noticed that at some particular times of the day and night, the traffic on Instagram is most prolific. Most users are online around nighttime as their daytime is usually filled with daily-life errands

and jobs. For different time zones, it is up to you to determine where the majority of your followers are from and accordingly time your posts so they reach as many users as possible. The more people see your posts, the more likes they are going to get. There are certain days of the week when more users are online and posting at times like this when the traffic is maximum may prove fruitful and get your profile the attention it deserves.

9. Don't do anything that may cause your followers to become annoyed and unfollow you. This could be because of bad quality photos or too much unimportant updates or too many pictures with the same content taken from different angles that spam the feeds of your followers. Rather, you should make a collage of all the differently angled photos and post them at once. Put some time between your posts, do not form a cluster and try to make sure your posts are all different from each other. This way your page is less likely to annoy the viewers.

10. Don't post too often. If you post too many pictures too soon, they may not get as many likes as they would have when posted only once or twice a day. Make use of the hash tags that describe the beauty of your pictures.

11. Bring a face into your pictures. It has been noticed that pictures with faces in them get more likes than the ones with no faces. When promoting products related to your business, you can have people pose with the products to get a greater amount of likes. If your business is related to the fashion industry, have models don the wearables and pose for the pictures.

12. Rather than using too many hash tags, it is recommended that you use only a few hash tags which are trending the most. Too many hash tags can make you look desperate for likes and that will make a bad impression. Instagram suggests to you the popular hash tags when typing, with the exact number of posts they have been used in.

13. Make smart use of your camera and the locations your pictures are set in. Good lighting, natural locations, sunrises and sunsets, clean background and other such factors are found to pique the interests of viewers and get more likes.

14. Use apps to track the activity of your account. There are a lot of them available in the app stores, for example Iconosquare and such. They can let you know about the activity of your followers as well, for example the time when they are most active and when you get the maximum amount of likes.

15. Color tints or hues of certain colors can make your photos look attractive. It is up to your judgment to decide which effects you want on your pictures.

16. Experiment with your pictures. You don't have to follow any strict line of action, rather try out new effects, angles and settings and come up with something unique. It may surprise your followers and capture their interest.

17. Take notes from other popular accounts relating to the same businesses as yours. Check out their most liked posts and find out what is it they are doing differently that makes them more appealing to the viewers. You

can implement the same to your own posts or develop something even better.

18. Don't post grainy and badly lit pictures. Use cameras with better resolution for photos. If the front facing camera of your mobile device is not as good, make use of the rear camera to take photos of yourself. Hire professionally efficient photographers if you need to.

19. Keep in mind that you do not want to change your picture so much from the original that it completely stops resembling the real thing. Keep the editing to a bare minimum; your posts may get more likes that way.

20. There's a story behind every picture. You can narrate the stories behind your posts in their respective captions. It may prove to be a good way to hold your followers' interest and gather more likes.

21. Be consistent in posting. Post regularly at the right intervals so your followers can expect when your next post is going to be.

22. Do not leave the queries and comments of your followers unattended. It may look like you do not appreciate your followers. Rather, you should make efforts to like their posts and reply to their comments appropriately. It will put you in their good books.

23. Build a theme for your account so people have an idea about the nature of your posts and what you have to offer. The theme of your profile should be according to your business whether it is food, fashion, travel or whatever else.

Chapter 5:

Making Profitable Posts

The main aim of a business on Instagram is to accumulate greater profits in the long run. Here's a rundown on how posts on Instagram can be utilized to do this. The pictures of the products that you upload should be very creative and the products should be highlighted.

A high-resolution picture should work just fine. If you have a business account, greater time and effort should be given in an effort to get the perfect pictures. Easy links should be provided for your followers so that they can view and purchase your products easily. If you post a particular product's picture, make sure you attach a direct link to the source or primary website where they can purchase it.

This is convenient for the potential customers and increases your chances of selling it. You should always describe your products in a creative but subtle way. Never be too direct or objective while writing a post. Let the product carry its own story. Make sure it is not bland and boring.

Never use a catalogue style of posting, where you only post the product and its price. The picture and description should act as a magnet to hook in the user so that they end up purchasing the product.

The Instagram Direct feature can be efficiently used to get in touch and interact with potential buyers. The conversations there are private and you can also send videos and pictures of the products via the direct-messaging feature.

You can get in touch with the active followers of your page through this and this helps in building up goodwill and brand loyalty. The followers will feel special and this in turn will convert them into loyal customers. Discounts and special offers are a necessity in order to gain popularity.

These offers enable you to gain more followers on Instagram and they will make it a point to follow your page, in the hope of getting more such offers. They are very effective and hold good for only the users who follow your account.

Similarly, **contests** are a useful way to attract more followers and make your brand known. If you host a contest or a giveaway event, it will be a nice way to engage your audience. Your account will get more traffic and your account's reach will automatically widen. The contest post should explicitly state the nature of the contest and the terms and conditions should be clearly mentioned.

You can either make a surprise gift or let it be known to the public what the gift is. The caption should instruct your followers on how to enter the contest. A lucky winner can then be chosen or you can add some more stipulations. It is a simple and efficient way to make your account known.

How to broaden your reach

Using Facebook

Your Instagram account will prosper if you link it with Facebook. Facebook has a huge user database and it will help get more likes for your posts. Advertisements and campaigns can be set up in order to generate interest and likes for the posts.

Your Facebook friends and likers will naturally converge at your Instagram page. Your presence on Instagram will be felt by everyone and they will eagerly wait for you to post more.

Using the Official Website of the Product

If you have a dedicated website for your product, then your Instagram account can be linked to it and promoted on the website. The website gets the most number of hits and this will help your Instagram account to grow.

Using E-mail

Emails are a very useful way of marketing your product. Email newsletters can be used to regularly keep your clients updated about the products. The Instagram account can be linked in your newsletter. Show your clients how active you are on Instagram and how it works as an efficient tool for your business.

This will give the users an idea of how they can benefit from Instagram as well.

Using Contests

Similarly, contests are a useful way to attract more followers and make your brand known. If you host a contest or a giveaway event, it will be a nice way to engage your audience. Your account will get more traffic and your account's reach will automatically widen. The contest post should explicitly state the nature of the contest and the terms and conditions should be clearly mentioned.

You can either make a surprise gift or let it be known to the public what the gift is. The caption should instruct your followers on how to enter the contest. A lucky winner can then be chosen or you can add some more stipulations. It is a simple and efficient way to make your account known.

Using hashtags

Users often search for images and content on basis of hash tags which define the categories of the product. You can always research and determine which hash tags are trending on Instagram and then use them in your posts. This will display your posts in the searches and help increase your reach. These hash tags easily attract likers and followers.

Chapter 6:

Marketing Tips For Instagram Business

The right tricks and tips of marketing should be used in order to accumulate enough profit and make your presence felt on Instagram. Here are some simple yet impacting marketing strategies.

- The primary feature of Instagram is photo sharing. Hence, you should focus on the quality and content of the photographs. Good quality pictures are more effective in sales. The better the quality is, the more likely it is to sell. Use various photo-editing applications and a good camera to take and enhance the pictures.

- Ads sponsored by Instagram are also great ways to enhance your business. Marketing a product requires some effort and the reach is comparatively limited. Sponsored ads that you pay for greatly increase the reach of your products and make your advertisement visible to any target audience. Hence investing in a sponsored advertisement is also a wise decision to make.

- The product bio should be strategic and creative. Direct links should be set up to direct users to your main website. Also strive to make this main website familiar with your followers. The main website should be identifiable with the users and they should have a feeling of satisfaction that the content is being directed towards them. The links can be modified in order to direct users towards any contest or special offers that you wish to engage them in.

- Helping other users and promoting their pages will subsequently help your page grow. If you promote other pages on your page, they will give your page a shout out in return, thus increasing your reach and followers. Helping them and getting factors in return can lead to a strong and beneficial relationship between you and them. This is easier when the nature and categories of your businesses are the same.

- Better engagement with your followers will lead to better connections with them. After connecting with them, persuade them to give you their email address and contact details. You can constantly keep them updated through emails and this makes you develop a personal connection with them. Keeping in touch with your followers is a very vital aspect of handling business on Instagram.

- Another way of increasing followers and likers is to pay for sponsored accounts. These accounts serve the sole purpose of helping other pages grow and widen their reach. These paid accounts have a huge base of followers who can directly see your products and get diverted to your page. It is a nice way to attract potential customers and increase the reach of a page.

- Getting in touch with real personalities who influence Instagram users is also a nice way to increase followers. If it is possible to contact them, you could connect with them and promote your products and contests. It is a sure shot way of attracting more followers. The influencer can then post about your product in a personal manner and thus influence followers towards your product. It is essential that they give a positive review of your product and tag your account in the description so that traffic can be directed to your account.

Instagram advertising

We have already discussed that Instagram has a paid advertising option. The following is a guide to using this service:

1) You will need to link your Instagram account to your Facebook account. Then the advertisement will be created by its Facebook Power Editor.

2) By going in the Settings tab, you can access the Instagram ads option. You can add your account from this section. You can login from this tab.

3) Next, select the type of advertisement that you need. There are three main objectives available and you can select any one of them. They are for clicks on your website, installing mobile apps or video views.

4) Then you need to choose an image ad, which will have a normal picture with a button that will re-direct the users to the page for clicks.

5) You then need to choose a video advertisement that will also have a re-directing button. It should be in video format though.

6) A carousel ad has multiple numbers of images, which a user can browse through. You can choose your ad depending on your style.

7) Your target audience can be determined when you have selected the kind of ad that you want. You can choose the location, gender, age and other aspects to refine your target audience. These are more detailed options to further limit your audience and help you get to the people whom you want to focus on. The right target audience can be a comprehensive game changer.

8) The advertisement content should be catchy and interesting, so as to hook in the audience. It should be clear in its message and not be ambiguous.

Advertisements should be used to maximum advantage. You could always ask others to mention your page in their posts and comments and use specific hash tags. A nice ad can boost your business in many ways. A good advertisement can improve your brand image and enhance your sales too.

Chapter 7:

Instagram Contests

You must be aware of the various contests and giveaways held by businesses on Instagram. There's always one or the other going on, and the prizes are lucrative. This isn't something new. It's been around on various platforms for quite a while now.

Nevertheless, it is still a powerful concept that can help you get positive results from your Instagram account. It generates substantial customer interest when executed properly and can be a quick way to attract and engage people with your brand.

In this chapter, let's discuss about the various types of Instagram contests and how you can use them to your advantage. The ways shown here are simple yet very effective.

Types of Instagram Contests

Let's first discuss the types of popular Instagram contest formats that you can choose from.

1) The simplest one is random in nature. You just ask your followers to like some specific post and give them a deadline. Once the deadline is past, you can go through all the users who have liked your post and then randomly

choose the winners from them. You can send these winners any of your own products, which most brands do, or you can send them some particular gift or subscription to a service. You can even give them discount coupons, either to your own stores or any other stores. This type of contest is a great way to gain a lot of followers and likes quickly.

2) Then the second type of contest is one in which you ask users to do some specific things. This usually includes uploading a particular type of photo and using a particular hashtag to go with that photo. The users upload a photo of the thing they've been asked to, use the hashtag, and tag the business' account to let them know about their participation. For example, if a brand that sells luxury gift items wants to boost its sales and visibility on Valentine's Day, it could start an Instagram contest telling users to upload photographs with their significant other, and use the hashtag #ValentinesDayContest for a chance to win amazing goodies from the said brand. People will then proceed to upload such photos and tag the brand's Instagram handle. After that, the next part is to choose the winning entries. This can be done randomly or on the basis of most likes received on the posts. Once the winners have been picked, you can tag them in a post or multiple posts and let them know what gifts they will be receiving. The great thing about such contests is that they're so easy to participate in that pretty much every potential customer who comes across it would participate. Uploading a photo is easy as pie, right?

3) Another ingenious way of attracting customers to your business is to ask them to click pictures at your official outlets or stores. This obviously doesn't work for businesses that don't have physical stores, but for the ones

that do, it can be really effective in luring people towards your stores. All you need to do is ask people to visit a store of your brand and click pictures there. Then you can ask them to upload the said photo(s) onto their own Instagram account with a relevant hashtag or you can do it through your brand's account. After the end of the contest, prizes can be distributed on the basis of the number of likes received on the users' photos. This allows you to engage your users both offline as well as online, and getting them inside your stores may even lead to increased sales. Make sure, however, that the contest doesn't go on for too long. A week or two is good enough as it ensures timely call to action from the potential customers.

4) Another thing you can do is to allow people to enter in the contests through your website as well as Instagram. This isn't difficult to do and increases your reach since many people may not have an Instagram account but may still want to participate in the contests. So giving them more options increases your chances of going viral.

5) Another type of contest is one in which you ask your customers to upload pictures or videos with your products. You can either ask them to simply pose with the product(s) or demonstrate how they like to use the product(s). Once they upload the photo or video, they need to put certain hashtags on it and tag your business's Instagram handle to let you know about their participation. This is one of the best marketing strategies when it comes to contests, since it shows a more intimate bond between the customers and your product(s). It focuses on your brand and the realness of it, since people get to witness actual, real users of your product(s). This strategy has recently become very popular among cosmetics and grooming product brands. You can see a lot of videos of people demonstrating how to use a

particular beard oil or shampoo, or how to apply a certain type of makeup. You can get tons of people interested in your product(s) through this strategy because not only does it give your current customers to be more loyal to your brand, it also attracts lots of new customers.

There are plenty of variations available for you to try and see what works best for you. Heck, you can even be creative and make your own type of contest. Mix and match, don't settle for average results. Always A/B test your strategies and analyze what's working best for you. This is what keeps your business ahead of others.

Instagram contests are a great way of attracting customers since everyone loves free gifts, and participating in contests is usually a very easy task, so most people find it very appealing. Remember, the traffic you generate is much more important than the money you spend on the prizes.

How to Hold a Successful Contest on Instagram?

Holding a successful contest on Instagram might feel like a massive task to you at first, but it's nothing our quick tips can't help you deal with.

1) The first thing you need to do is set a proper objective or goal for your contest. You want to achieve this goal by the end of your contest and the contest needs to be driven with this purpose if you want to get positive results.

2) Once the objective is set, you need to think about your target audience. You should have a good idea about the people you want to reach through your contest. That is how you will frame your contest, so it appeals to those

particular people. If you try to create a contest that appeals to everyone, you will end up attracting no one.

3) Once the goal of your contest and your target audience has been decided, you want to think about the details of your contest next.

4) The first thing you want to decide is the prize you are going to give away, since that's one of the most important parts of the contest. Without attractive prizes, you can't hope to draw in customers and hold their attention. If you can't make people want to participate in your contest, there is no point to holding it. So set an appropriate budget, and keeping that in mind, decide the prizes that you're going to be giving away to your contest's winners.

5) Once you've settled on the prizes, you need to create a beautiful and attention grabbing post that will announce the start of your contest. Regardless of how awesome the prizes are, if the post can't grab the attention of people it's supposed to, the contest will be rendered useless. So make sure your announcement post is attention-worthy. You can choose to show people the potential prizes, too, if you think that will get them going.

6) We've already talked about the different types of contests that can be held on Instagram. You can choose from them or create your own by mixing and matching your favorite bits. The point is to reach the highest number of potential customers that you can through your contest, so you need to keep them in mind while deciding the type of contest you want to hold. For example, if your brand sells women's handbags, it's a good idea to ask women to upload photos with your bags on their Instagram handles. Create a unique theme if possible and use it, and make sure the

hashtag you ask the users to add to their photos is unique and catchy enough. That's one way to make sure your contest gains traction.

7) If you're wondering why the use of a special hashtag is so important for your contest, let me tell you about the power of hashtags. They are used to track posts because they act as a sort of search function. All the posts that use a particular hashtag can be viewed by searching for that hashtag. This is why these hashtags are so popular on all sorts of social media. This is how things get to be classed as "trending." So to manage your contest better, you need to ask all participants to use a unique hashtag you've created for your contest. It also helps to have your brand's Instagram account tagged in all such posts so you can acknowledge them when they're made.

8) Another thing you need to keep in mind is to create some rules for the contest and only consider the entries of participants who're within the rules of the contest. Obviously, one of the first rules should be that the participant should be following your brand's Instagram handle.

9) Make sure you stay up to date with all the entries flowing in for your contest and keep interacting with your fans by tracking the hashtag you've asked them to use. Having a unique hashtag helps you create a community around the contest because no other brand or activity can take away from your efforts. People who've entered in your contest get noticed with ease and find it easy to look for other participants' entries in turn.

10) Setting a deadline for your contests is also very important. The period for which the contest runs depends on the scale and type of contest it is. Some people like to regularly hold weekly or fortnightly contests to keep traffic flowing in to their websites. It's usually a low investment operation and so, the prizes also don't have to be anything over the top. It's just something to keep your current followers busy for the most part. But when there's a special occasion and you're holding a bigger contest where the stakes are higher and the prizes are also more valuable, you know you have to set the deadline accordingly. You want your customers to actually work for it, so you can set some different rules for such contests and set a longer deadline for them. Make sure, however, that you always let your customers know how the winners are going to be chosen. Whatever criteria it is that you decide upon for choosing the winner(s), be clear about it and convey it to your audience. You don't want any conflict or confusion, as it will hurt your goodwill.

11) After you've held a few contests, you will have a fair amount of experience with the analytics of it all. You have seen the response from the users, and you have determined the profitability of it all. After this, you can easily decide how often and on what scale you want to hold these contests. If you see that a lot of traffic is coming to your brand from these contests, go on and take it to the next level. However, if you don't seen much response, it's time to rethink your strategy and hold back a little so you can plan more and execute your contests better.

12) An important thing to do once you've started the contest is to promote it on as many platforms as possible. So make sure you let your followers on Twitter, Facebook, and other social media platforms know that you're holding a

contest. Announce it on your website and your blog, too. Moreover, you can even make some arrangement with a few thought leaders and influencers in your industry to talk about your contest on their own social media platforms. Ads on Facebook and Twitter are also a great way to increase visibility of your contests. If the prizes are worth it, people from all platforms will come flocking to your Instagram to participate.

13) Don't forget to monitor your contests once they're up and running. Google Analytics, Twitter alerts, etc. are some really useful third party tools that you can use to track the progress of your contests and see the amount of traffic you're converting.

14) When the contest ends and you announce the winner(s), make sure you contact them and tell them the great news. You can announce it on your Instagram with a nice post, but there's something even better you can do. You can send them the prize and ask them to send you a photo of them with the prize. Then you can upload that photo on your Instagram account. This gives a more intimate feel to your contest and people become much more interested in participating in your contests in the future.

If you follow these tips, you will surely succeed in creating and executing amazing contests for your Instagram audience!

Chapter 8:

External Tools

If recent studies are to be believed, social media is an integral part of most brands' success, and successful brands try to be active on as many platforms as possible. It has been shown that Instagram can boost the engagement of the businesses with their respective audiences by as much as 30% more than any other social media website. You can imagine how big that figure is.

Using Instagram, however, is not as simple as you would expect. It requires knowledge of certain things they don't tell you everywhere. In this chapter, we take a look at some great third party tools that you can use to boost your Instagram experience and use it to a much bigger advantage than the average Instagram user. Let's begin.

Instagress

So your business is growing steadily and so is your Instagram following. It's starting to get really difficult to keep track of all the notifications and messages, and to respond to them all in time. You're not large enough to hire social media managers but can't afford to miss responding to any followers either! This sure is a tough situation. Well, worry not; Instagress is here to help you with that!

Instagress is basically an automation software that puts your Instagram account on a bit of an autopilot, giving you superpowers. But be careful how you use them! You don't want to get banned, do you? As long as you maintain a human touch to your messages and your autopilot behavior, you'll be good.

Let's take a look at the various features of Instagress.

- **Comments** – Instagress can comment for you. This means you can program Instagress to comment certain things on certain types of posts. You can do this on the basis of hashtags. Make sure the comments sound catchy and not generic. You can even check an option so that the app doesn't comment the same thing on multiple posts by the same user.

- **Advanced filters** – This feature lets you get a bit specific with your audience. There are a lot of settings to choose from and as long as you make a smart filter, Instagress will have a pretty good list of users to work with.

- **Followers** – With the help of Instagress, you can automatically follow people that are following a particular account. This means that those people will notice you and they might even follow you back if they're interested in your brand. For example, athletes do this a lot on Instagram so they can attract potential sponsors.

- **Tags** – You can even set Instagress to use certain tags in your Instagram posts automatically. This helps in promoting your posts and getting them more visibility. But even here, you have to be careful about the kind of hashtags you use. You want to avoid spam hashtags that are often used by spammers. Keep updating your hashtag list from time to time and set up your 'blacklist' so your Instagress knows what tags to avoid using.

There's much more that Instagress can do for you, but you need to be careful with it. It's a robot that doesn't think for itself and will follow only what you command it to do. So make sure your Instagram account seems human and doesn't appear spammy to anyone.

You don't want to be flagged for being a bot. With cautious use, Instagress can be one of the absolute best marketing tools for you!

Iconosquare

Your marketing plan must be bigger than just Instagram. There needs to be a proper strategy and a theme around which you base your whole marketing efforts. If that isn't present, you have no plan and no achievable goals at all.

What you want out of Instagram is for it to contribute well in your overall marketing plan, and this needs to be monitored by you on a regular basis. If you can't check how it's affecting your larger plan, there's no use to running an Instagram account.

You need to be able to know at a second's glance how many followers you have gained or lost in a period of time, what the reasons behind it are, and how much traffic you're generating to your blog or website through Instagram.

Iconosquare lets you do all this by providing you important insights and data about follower behavior. You can then break down everything into small sections and look deeper into them. All the metrics you need are right at your fingertips and you can look at everything that has been affecting your account's progress. With this information, you can correct yourself when you think you're going wrong.

Let's take a look at some of the main features of Iconosquare.

- **Analytics** – This is pretty much the prime function of Iconosquare. It helps the user understand important facts and figures with such ease that one can't help but be awed. There are graphs and charts and the whole shebang. Iconosquare will give you all the important details you need and then some!

- **Web view** – Instagram is a mobile app, so there's not much scope for multiple viewing experiences. The screen options are limited, even if you're browsing it on a laptop computer. This can make the whole experience boring and maybe even a bit frustrating sometimes. Iconosquare provides you a multifaceted view of the app in which you can manage your own viewing preferences. You can keep a record of all the people you've ever interacted with. Not only that, you can arrange your feed by likes, comments, pictures, and much more.

- **Audience engagement** – Like Twitter, Instagram is also an open platform, which means if you have a public account, anyone can interact with your posts. This can result in really messy comment threads. You don't want to end up missing half the comments you should be responding to. This is where Iconosquare helps you be ordered.

- **Contests** – We've already talked about how important contests are and how you can host one. Iconosquare has inbuilt features that can help you successfully create and host contests on Instagram, too!

Schedugram

This is another amazing tool that helps you use your Instagram account with much more ease. Over the years, Schedugram has proven itself to be a solid marketing tool for people who use Instagram widely. It has helped many businesses gain visibility at very affordable prices.

Let's take a look at some of its features.

- The main feature, as the name suggests, is to be able to schedule posts for later. You can create a schedule for your Instagram account and posts will be made on your behalf at the exact time you want them to be. This automates a lot of things and reduces your responsibility of checking and handling the account all day. You can even keep the account active when you're asleep, so people from other time zones can interact with your brand.

- You can use Schedugram with multiple Instagram accounts. It's easy as pie and switching between accounts is a complete breeze.

- In Schedugram, you can even share your Instagram account with multiple people so they can access it any time. This is very important for businesses where multiple users may be posting through the same account at different times of the day. You can also manage permissions and responsibilities, which is pretty awesome.

Websta

Another really popular analytics tool for Instagram, earlier called Webstagram, it can help you study the latest trends in the app so you always stay updated and use the best hashtags. It used to be a simple web viewer for the mobile app, Instagram, but is now much more than that.

Let's see some of its features.

- **Gallery Widget** – Turn any feed you have (hashtag, location, profile, anything) into a beautiful gallery and display it on your website or blog!

- **Websta Board** – Helps you organize your posts into groups and categories so you can manage them better.

- **Search** – Get statistics on the most popular hashtags by searching for them and use them in your own posts.

- **Sharing** – This feature lets you easily share content on Websta and other platforms.

- **Visitors** – This feature lets you see who is visiting your website and how it affects your account.

- **My Stats** – This lets you check all statistics related to your account and posts.

Chapter 8: External Tools

These are just some of the third party tools available for use on the web to help augment your Instagram experience. Try them out and see what works for you. You don't have to use them all, because in the end, each business is different and has different needs. Just make sure you keep testing and analyzing what works best for you.

Conclusion

With this, we have reached the end of this book. I hope you enjoyed reading it as much as I enjoyed writing it!

It has been an absolute pleasure teaching you about the basics of Instagram and how you can use it to boost your business performance. There is a lot of information in this book, so take it one step at a time and make sure to practically test everything at each step. That's how you learn and improve!

Thank you for reading this book and I hope your Instagram account turns into a huge win for your business!

I would highly appreciate if you could leave me a review of this book on Amazon. I like to hear feedback and am open ears to hear how I can make this book even better. Cheers!

www.ingramcontent.com/pod-product-compliance
Lightning Source LLC
Chambersburg PA
CBHW071820170526
45167CB00003B/1385